FROM THE
RAT RACE
TO THE
GOD RACE

How To Live The Purpose Driven
Life God Has For You.

By
Daniel Olugbenga Mateola

FROM THE RAT RACE TO THE GOD RACE
Published by

Daniel Olugbenga Mateola
Perazim International Christian Centre
820 S. Central Ave, Medford OR 97501
Email: info@danielmateolaministries.org
Websites: www.perazimchurch.org; www.danielmateola.org

ISBN-13: 978-1475257465
ISBN-10: 1475257465

Manufactured in the United States

Library of Congress CIP data applied for.
9 8 7 6 5 4 3 2 1 0
FIRST PRINTING: May 2012

Pastor Daniel brilliantly provides a strong metaphor to illustrate a revelation and a timely message for getting out of the "rat race" into the joy and abundance of "God's race". Jesus promises that as we seek and make Him and the kingdom of God principles our priority, that, "all these things shall be added to you". I highly recommend this book to every person seeking a better understanding of how to operate in God's plan and purpose for their lives.

Pastor Tayo Jaiyeola
Founding President
Believers Faith Ministry Tennessee, USA

This is a must read for anyone who wants to break free from the rat race into a life one of purpose and true fulfillment. Be edified, encouraged, and empowered as you meditate and digest the truth espoused in this book.

Bishop (Dr.) Mike Zino
Founder & Senior Pastor
Glory & Peace Church Int. Winnipeg. Canada

What a very apt and accurate word. It is a rat race when we follow the herd and not step aside to listen to the voice of the Holy Spirit. I trust God that as you read this book, the Holy Spirit will open your heart and your life to follow God's race for your life and that you may run the race with patience to win it all and receive a crown of victory in Jesus Christ.

Pastor Daniel Mateola's book is a clarion call and an encouragement even in these times not to be discouraged or dismayed because of the times, but to muster up courage and faith to follow after God. I love books that preach faith that anchors our belief systems in the Lord and that is what this author is doing, preaching a powerful message of faith anchored in God and His promises.

Dr. Hezekiah Adesanya
Bishop
Reconciliation Ministries World Outreach.

"From Rat Race to God Race" is a God inspired revelation for the body of Christ today. It contains deep insights into how scriptures confirm how believers in Jesus are to live today and using the principles shared in this book can be the difference between life of mediocrity and life of purpose; it can be the difference between getting-by in life and really enjoying this God given life; it can be the difference between a life of misery and that of joy.

Niyi Olujobi
Senior Pastor
RCCG House of Praise, Essex, United Kingdom

CONTENTS

DEDICATION

To God be the glory, great things He has done.
This book is dedicated to my number one helper of destiny
– my wife – whom God has used to encourage me to
discover my God race and to keep on running.

ACKNOWLEDGEMENTS

To my wife, Ruth Adetilewa Mateola, I want to say thank you for coming into my life in 1994 at a time when I lacked purpose and direction. You have inspired and encouraged me to mature as a man, husband, father and pursue my life purpose. Thank you for blessing me with our wonderful son Jeremiah and our beautiful daughters Jeiel and Destiny.

To my parents, Mr. Akinbowale Mateola & Mrs. Christianah Mateola, thank you for giving me sound education and a strong foundation in life. You have deposited in me the knowledge and fear of God which has helped shape my life and character. Consider this book as one of the fruits of your labor.

To my children, Jeremiah, Jeiel and Destiny, thank you for being good children and not overwhelming me with too much that I am able to serve God, His people and even to get the chance to write.

Special thanks to Lynn Campbell, Abi Adewunmi and Alex Starla Reynolds for the editorial work. I also want to appreciate the entire PICC church family for being a wonderful congregation.

FOREWORD

Someone once said at the heart of the matter is the matter of the heart. Everything we do in life flows out from the cradle of our hearts. Therefore to change our lives, we need to shift inwardly. This is the basic principle of true transformation where we morph from the inside out. Too many people are trapped by their inner world which needs real spiritual climate change.

I would like to pose a question. Would you plan for the next twenty years (assuming you had that) or rather for the next one million years of your life? Do you realize that you are still going to be alive in some form in the next one billion years? The craziness of it all is that so called believers who know about eternity are doing their best to ignore it. By staying stuck in the rat race of life, you'll end up trading in all the blessings and riches of eternity for pittance in this life.

Let me elaborate with a ridiculous illustration. A young city broker pulls off the deal of the century and is awarded six billion dollars in cash. The money is delivered by six trucks to his mansion and loaded into the mega vault amidst tight security. As the delivery entourage begins to leave his house he sees a mint one dollar bill stuck to the side of one of the Lorries. He shouts to the driver to stop but they cannot hear him so he runs downstairs in haste, in his pajamas! He hits the driveway just in time as the six wheeler pulls out. The dollar bill is still stuck to the lorry. He is determined to get that one dollar so he jumps unto the back vender of the truck as it speeds off. He clings on for dear life and stretches to grab the note flapping in the wind. The lorry swerves unto the freeway with the billionaire hanging on trying to grab his money. Just as he touches it, his foot slips and he falls headfirst unto the tarmac and two vehicles slam into him breaking almost every bone in his body. He is rushed to hospital and straight to the intensive care unit. He is alive but strung up with plaster all over his body and tubes coming out of everywhere.

Does this sound too bizarre or ludicrous? Think deeply about it. So many of us are ardently determined to grab that one note whilst ignoring the vast wealth that is already ours. Do you realize that compared to the vastness of eternity and what God has given us in Christ, our vanities are like that one dollar? When we stand in eternity and look back on our lives, then we will see how incomparable the blessings of Heaven are to this life.

The volume you hold in your hand contains downloadable truths and principles that will help reshape your perspective, priorities and will cause you to hunger to run your God ordained race all the way to the finish line. May you truly be free from the rat race and enter into your God race.

Pastor Jonathan Oloyede
Founder & President
Global Day of Prayer London.

INTRODUCTION

There are two kinds of workers in this world. Everyone falls into one of these two categories. Group one are the people that work just for the money they can make. Their paycheck is their main motivation. Group two are the people who work to fulfill their passion and purpose. These two groups of people are not just working with different motives; they are also working for two different masters. Let's review these two groups of workers further.

Working primarily for a paycheck, people in group one tend to have the mentality that they are working for man. Those belonging in group one have the tendency to do the least amount of work possible to receive their paycheck by doing the bare minimum. On the other hand, those in group two have the mentality of working for themselves or for God, so they tend to put more effort into what they do.

People in group one also tend to work jobs just to make money unlike those in group two who will only do what they know they are passionate about. This is why many in group one tend to hate their job. Statistically it is said that most Americans hate their jobs but have no choice than to wake up every morning to go to the same job they hate. Unlike group one, group two loves their work as it brings out their ingenuity, creativity and personality. They are absolutely passionate about what they do. As a matter of fact, when you speak to most people in group two, they will tell you that they don't even consider what they do as work. Some enjoy what they do so much that they can even do it without pay.

Another important thing to highlight is that most people in group one tends not to become rich. It's hard to become rich doing something you hate. Many in this group work until they reach retirement age, hoping their pension and savings will sustain them in their latter years. On the other hand, people in group two tend to become the wealthy people in our society. Their passion, creativity, and ingenuity usually cause them to excel in what they do ultimately bringing great financial rewards as well as recognition.

Those in group one are usually stuck in what I call "The Rat Race" where they are always working hard, trying to meet their needs. As the needs never seem to be fully met, they have to go back and work a little harder each time, never really getting ahead. The second group usually gets out of *the rat race* and ends up fulfilling their life's passion and purpose. This second group is where God wants His children to be. This is why Jesus made the statement about the mammon system in Matthew 6:24. He warned his disciples to not let this system become their master because the mammon system is notorious for keeping God's people in *the rat race*. Thus, they never truly fulfill the plan and purpose God has for their lives. I want you to know that there is more to your life than just working jobs. You too can live a life of purpose and fulfillment. You just need to know how to get from wherever you're at now to this place of a fulfilling life. In essence, you just need to know how to get from group one to group two.

Just about a decade ago, I came to the realization that I was in "The Rat Race." I owned and ran a small information technology consulting firm in London, England that did well financially, yet I was unfulfilled. The key problem was that I worked hard weekly to make money which I spent on bills and some luxuries to fill the vacuum in my heart that was caused by my lack of fulfillment. I had known I had a call on my life to preach God's word and impact lives for Him, but had no clue on how to make the transition from what I was doing to becoming a preacher.

One of the issues I was facing was possible financial collapse if I quit my rat race.

Today, as I write this book, I am glad to let you know that I am in my "God Race"; doing only what I enjoy without financial trouble. A couple of years ago the Lord led me to start documenting the principles He had taught me which led me on my journey out of "The Rat Race" and into my "God Race." This book has been written to communicate these principles as well as the heart of God for His children with regards to how we live our lives for Him. What matters is not the duration of your life but the donation of your life. It is my desire that you will learn profound truths which will help you to get out of "The Rat Race" and into your "God Race" of passion, purpose and personal destiny.

Chapter 1

PARADIGM SHIFTS

"And do not be conformed to this world, but be transformed by the renewing of your mind, that you may prove what is that good and acceptable and perfect will of God."

Romans 12:2 (NKJV)

What is a Paradigm? My favorite definition for this word "paradigm" is found in Webster's dictionary. It states that a paradigm is: *a philosophical and theoretical framework of a scientific school or discipline within which theories, laws, and generalizations and the experiments performed in support of them are formulated.* This simply means that a man's paradigm is the framework of his thinking or mindset. It affects how he processes information with regards to specific issues. For example, a man that was raised in poverty and has never had enough in his lifetime has the tendency to believe that there isn't enough supply of anything in the world. This becomes his paradigm and how he views any issue regarding the supply of resources. I call it a "lack mentality." This person can be so deceived by this "lack mentality" that he never tries to get more than enough of anything. The framework of lack is a reflection of this person's paradigm. Now let's imagine for a moment that this person is invited to a seminar where a speaker is motivating people to believe for increase, prosperity or abundant supply. The natural tendency of this person, with the lack mentality or paradigm, is to reject the words of the speaker. He might even walk out in the middle of the seminar claiming the speaker is unrealistic. The truth is that unless the man is willing to change his paradigm, he cannot benefit from the seminar. This is what I refer to as a "paradigm shift."

Our paradigms have all been shaped by our experiences in life. We have all been born and raised in different homes, by different parents, in different neighborhoods, cities and even nations. This is the reason why we all tend to see things from varying perspectives. Everyone's perspective is ultimately based on their own paradigms including Christian perspectives. The day you give your heart to Jesus and become saved, your mindset and paradigms do not immediately change. As a matter of fact, the older a person is before they get saved, the more difficult it is to experience paradigm shifts. There is a tendency to think that what you have believed from your life experiences is the gospel truth.

"…making the word of God of no effect through your tradition which you have handed down. And many such things you do."
Mark 7:13

Mindsets or paradigms can also be developed based on the culture with which a person is raised. This is when people automatically do certain things in certain ways because that is how it is done in their culture. This is what Jesus was trying to deal with when He made the statements in Mark 7:13 as quoted above. At that time, people were treating their parents in a way based on culture and traditions contrary to the statutes and preferences of God. Today, many of us Christians are guilty of the same thing. We do things in certain ways based on our culturally influenced paradigms. It's time for change! According to Paul, the way to ensure that you are not conforming to the world is to be ready to renew your mind with the Word of God. This simply means you need to stay flexible when it comes to embracing a paradigm shift that is necessary, based on new found truth in God's word.

In this book there are certain truths the Lord has revealed to me that will require you to allow yourself to experience paradigm shifts. You have to be willing to give up your old thinking framework or paradigms in order to embrace the new, based on God's word. Many people are stuck in *the rat race* because of their unwillingness to change. If you are one of those people, I strongly appeal for you to make a decision to change before you continue reading this book. I urge you to stop now and say to yourself, "I am willing to shift my paradigm whenever I encounter truth from God's word that is different from what I have believed so that I may embrace my future in God." I pray that God's grace will be available to you to do just that!

Nothing Changes Until Your Thinking Changes

I once heard someone say, "Insanity is when a person keeps doing the same thing in the same way over again expecting a different result each time." The truth is that nothing changes in our lives until we change. Another person said, "Change is not change until you change." It is important to also understand that you will not change any action or deed unless you first change your mindset concerning that action or deed. The reason why people do not change what they are doing, even when it is wrong, is because they have yet to believe that what they are doing is wrong. Thus, we have to be careful about what we consider as Christian conversion.

A person is not really saved until they have had the opportunity to reflect on their past deeds and repent of their sinful ways. A person is not saved because they prayed the sinner's prayer; rather, they are saved because they mean the words of the sinners prayer which they have prayed. As a matter of fact, the true meaning of the word "repent" is to change your mind. In other words, you have considered your actions and realized that you have been wrong and need to change your actions. Consequently, I believe the reason why some in the church today are still living in the same sins they were indulging in before is because although they prayed the sinner's prayer they have not truly repented of the sinful ways of their past. Honestly! They are not yet saved. Only true repentance activates God's grace that empowers a new Christian to live a righteous life.

I encourage you, once again, to be ready to make the necessary mindset changes or paradigm shifts as you encounter the truth which will be revealed to you in this book. Understand that your results will change only after your actions have changed. Your actions will change only after you have changed your mind. It is time you renew your mind for a good change!

Prayer:

Lord, I thank You that I am made in Your image and after Your likeness. I thank You I have the mind of Christ and thus the capacity to see things and receive truths based on Your perspective. I repent of my past sinful works based on faulty mindset or paradigms. Now I pray that You will renew my mind to be in synch with Your Word and Your plans for my life…my destiny. In Jesus Name! Amen (so be it)!

Chapter 2

THE RAT RACE

*"I went in response to a revelation and, meeting privately with those esteemed as leaders; I presented to them the gospel that I preach among the Gentiles. I wanted to be sure I was not running and had not been **running my race in vain**."*

Galatians 2:2 (NIV)

In my introduction, I mentioned that many Christians will not be able to fulfill their God ordained purpose and destiny because they are currently stuck in a *rat race*. One reason why many will remain stuck is that they do not know they are in a *rat race*. Some do not even know there is anything like a *rat race* or what it really looks like.

What Is The Rat Race?

I did some study on this term "rat race" to discover how it came about and how best to define it. One author defines "The Rat Race" as: *fierce competition in the work place.*

He said it is about working hard to try to maintain or improve one's positions in the work place or social standing. Hence you are in a type of *rat race* when you are continually trying to keep or improve your standard of life but never really succeeding. Someone else defines the term "rat race" as: *an endless, self-defeating and pointless pursuit.* The term was originally coined by some scientists doing experiments with rats in a laboratory. The rats were put into a maze and left to run around, thinking they were going somewhere, but they were never really going anywhere. They also designed a type of wheel for the rats to run on, which worked just like a treadmill. No matter how hard the rats ran, they remained in the same spot not going anywhere. All the rats got on this wheel was good exercise. Personally, I believe you are in "The Rat Race" when your hard work does not really result in progress with regards to where you want to go in life. It is like working at a job, continually, just to spend all your income meeting needs. Then needing to go back and do it over and over again, with no real gain.

Most people who have lived and worked long enough realize what they once thought were truths, are really myths. There are two myths most people believe in life concerning their work or careers. One myth is: "Work your job really hard and you will obtain wealth. Then one day, you won't have to work anymore and can spend the rest of your life enjoying your passion." I have discovered that people who just work for money (*i.e.* group one), never really get to that place of wealth accumulation. They discover, as the years go by, that they need to continue working if they are going to be able afford to meet their needs.

The second myth is: "If you give forty or fifty years of your life to your job, one day you'll retire with a pension large enough to live on and pursue your passion, never having to work again." This is indeed a myth as it's not always the case for many who have worked those numbers of years with that expectation. If you don't believe it, just take a trip to your local Wal-Mart or grocery store and you will find many people, past retirement age, still working. I understand that there are some seniors working just to keep busy. However, I can assure you that most of the ones we see everyday are working in order to meet their needs. These seniors, at some point before or after retirement age, discovered that they did not have enough to pursue their passion and enjoy the rest of their lives.

History Of The Rat Race

As I continued to study this subject, the Spirit of the Lord made me realize that, historically, man has not always been in a *rat race*. In the bible days, most men had occupations like farming food crops or rearing animals. Others were carpenters or blacksmiths. Their work was based on their God given skills or talents, which many times were passed down through generations to meet the needs of their families. We don't have to go back very far in history to find this generational transfer.

Personally, I can look back to three generations of my own family and see that my great-grandparents were not in "The Rat Race." I am talking about a time when people would go out and get their own logs and clay to build their homes. They built it themselves. Nobody took out a mortgage to own a home, so no one owed anyone. If you were a tailor, and everyone knew you as a tailor, people paid you for your work and it was enough to take care of your family. Life was simple and maintaining it was basic. There was no need for anyone to get into *the rat race*. Historically, most people were more interested in the provision of what they would eat, the clothes they would put on and the roof over their heads. Life was indeed simple.

I remember when I was studying economics in high school. I learned that there was a time when money was not used as a means of exchange. Instead, to obtain what one needed, it was done as a "trade-by-barter." Trade-by-barter means that if I was a farmer raising chickens and wanted to eat some yams or potatoes, I would take some of my chickens to the trade-by-barter market. Then I would look for someone who wanted chickens in exchange for their yams or potatoes. That was how needs were met. If I needed some work done by the blacksmith, I would take my chickens to him. I would offer to give him some chickens in exchange for his work. If I needed a table, I would take my chickens to the carpenter.   Life was simple then.

Increased Lust For Things & The Debt Trap

Along the way, two things were introduced to mankind. Those two things became a part of what put mankind into this rat maze of entrapment. One of the two was an increase of lust for material things. When life focused on eating, clothing and a roof over one's head, it was all very easy. But life in the 21st century is much more complicated. There are so many things we desire. In order to have all these material "things," we end up entering into this maze trying to make money so we can afford to pay for it all.

Today, a Christian who just bought a house or car gladly shares this testimony with fellow congregants as a blessing from the lord. Though a new house could be a good testimony, it could also become something that keeps you running around in the rat maze. This is true when you borrow more than you can afford in order to pay the house you just bought. Remember that you also need to spend money monthly to maintain that new house. Another interesting discovery about this generation with increased lust for material things is that the lust is rarely satisfied. People easily get tired of the things they recently acquired and soon start longing for something new.

Helping to facilitate entrapment in *the rat race*, the second thing mankind was introduced is the debt system. Historically, there was a time many necessities such as houses and means of transportation were not financed. Most people saved up to get whatever they needed or wanted and gladly did without anything they could not afford.

Unfortunately, today our increased lust for things has facilitated the massive growth of the financial debt system – cause and effect. I believe this debt system is one of satan's greatest weapons holding mankind in bondage. He entices us by saying, "Enjoy today and pay later." It is easy to some, under the illusion, to think they can afford what they really cannot. If one really could afford it, one would have saved up and bought it outright. Our forefathers used to do it that way. They saved up to get the things they needed or wanted. Every time you choose to buy something today with intent to pay later, you are agreeing to lock yourself up in *the rat race* for x-number of months or even years. Delayed gratification is a sign of maturity.

Many Christians today know what the Lord has purposed for them to accomplish in life, but cannot do it because they are stuck in *the rat race*. You do not want to wake up every day of your life just to get back into *the rat race* in order to pay for all the "things" you've acquired but could not afford. The house mortgage, the car payment and that 90 inch flat screen TV. Let's hope you enjoy it to the max, because it is keeping you in "The Rat Race" and out of "The God Race."

These "things" are what is making your life so complicated. So much so, it is no longer easy to get out. The danger, at this point is that even when you work hard and your boss gives you a raise, there is a natural tendency to increase your standard of living, rather than to pay off what you already owe. Many, by exchanging their old car with a new one, end up keeping themselves stuck in *the rat race*.

I truly believe that this *rat race* is one of satan's greatest weapons to keep Christians from fulfilling their

God ordained purpose in life. The great men and women of God in the bible would have never accomplished what they did for Him if they had been stuck in *the rat race.*

Imagine the Apostle Paul in the prayer meeting of Acts chapter thirteen, hearing the Spirit of the Lord speak, saying, *"...Separate unto Me Paul and Barnabas for I have an assignment for them..." and* after hearing the prophetic word saying, "Sorry guys, I can't go. I have a house payment and a car payment, so God; you'll have to find someone else." Think about it for a moment. You know the reason Paul could get up and say, "Alright Barnabas, let's get out of here! Let's go take the cities for Jesus!" was because there was nothing holding them down.

In Acts chapter 2, one of the first miracles the Lord did for the early church was that of debt freedom. In Acts 2:44 the Bible states, *"...all who believed were together, an*d *had all things in common..."* Continuing in verse 45, *"And sold their possessions and goods and parted them to all men, as every man had need."* The apostles distributed the possessions according to every person's needs. The Holy Spirit moved in the hearts of the wealthy Christians to sell their lands and bring their money to the apostles. They in turn used the money to set all the other believers free from debt.

The early church started with everyone having their needs met and consequently they all got out of debt. The kingdom of God was preached by men and women who were free from *the rat race* and could go do the work of the Lord. Every man that wants to do something great for God in their life time must get out and stay out of "The Rat Race."

Prayer:

Father, I repent for my sins of greed and lust for material things that have caused me to become trapped in the rat race. I ask for your divine help to get out as quickly as possible in Jesus Name. Give me wisdom of what to do and the grace to act upon it. I reject lack, poverty and debt from my life and family. I pray to receive my portion of the riches that Jesus shed His blood to purchase for me, in Jesus Name…Amen!

Is There A Way Out?

Chapter 3

IS THERE A WAY OUT OF THE MAZE?

"Behold, I will do a new thing, Now it shall spring forth; Shall you not know it? I will even make a road in the wilderness and rivers in the desert."

Isaiah 43:19 (NKJV)

One thing every child of God must understand about our Abba is that He is the God of possibilities. There is never anything too hard for Him to fix or anything too jammed up for Him to make a way out. According to Isaiah, God is capable of making a road way right in the middle of a wilderness and cause rivers to spring up in the middle of the desert. Our God is The Pro at making a way where there seems to be no way. The main criteria, is that you have to believe there is a way out and then be willing to pay the necessary price to get out to your land of freedom.

Dealing With Hopelessness

If you have ever experienced a tough challenge in life, you will understand how easy it is to get into a state of hopelessness. As a matter of fact, satan specializes in helping people to get to a road called "hopelessness." He is so good at painting a picture that your challenge is so special no one else could have ever experienced such a challenge. This is why one of my favorite bible verses is 1 Corinthians 10:13 (NKJV):

"No temptation has overtaken you except such as is common to man; but God is faithful, who will not allow you to be tempted beyond what you are able, but with the temptation will also make the way of escape, that you may be able to bear it."

The first thing I want you to note in this powerful statement Paul made is the word "temptation." This comes from the Greek word "peirasmos" which means: *an experiment or trial or proving.* It also means "an adverse condition."

The second thing I want you to note is the first sentence in that thirteenth verse, *"No temptation has overtaken you except such as is common to man."* Here Paul is categorically stating that there is no trial or adverse condition you will go through that is so special no one else has ever experienced it. In other words, someone else has been through the worst problem or trial that you could ever experience. This thought should give you hope that there is a way out.

What you need to ask yourself is: "Has anyone else survived a similar situation? If so, how did they survive it or overcome the adversity?" As soon as you start thinking in the light of this truth stated by Paul, you will realize there is no need for you to stay parked on the road called "hopelessness."

Now you understand why satan and his agents try hard to convince you that you are the only one going through your situation or that yours is unique compared to what others have experienced. And, I hope you understand that this is a lie from the pits of hell. If you feel your trial is special, it is because you made it so yourself by allowing satan to rule in that area of your life.

If you take a closer look at the second sentence in verse 13 of 1Corinthians 10, you will see that Paul also stated that God is faithful not to allow you to be presented with a trial that is beyond your capacity to handle. In other words, whatever you are allowed to face is not big enough to wipe you out. You can handle it! This is another reason why you cannot accept the feeling of hopelessness. Stop for a moment to confess the following: "*I am not hopeless! I can handle whatever trial God has permitted me to face and I shall surely come out of it victorious!*"

Another trick of the enemy to keep you on "the road of hopelessness" is to convince you to be secretive about your trial. He will try to convince you that you will be mocked and ridiculed by those you might go to for help, particularly if the trial has to do with sin and/or compromise. I urge you do not to fall for this trick. With regards to *the rat race*, you will be shocked to find out that there are more people stuck in the same or similar situation with you than those who are free.

Today, many have learned to give false impressions of their financial condition. I call it "false prosperity." I urge you to become hungry in finding the solution to your challenges which are trying to keep you stuck in the muck. You are not hopeless!

Quest For Wisdom

One of my favorite definitions for wisdom is: *"Knowing what to do when you have a challenge."* Wisdom is not the same thing as knowledge. To have wisdom is to know when to apply the relevant knowledge in order to solve the particular challenge you are facing at any point in time.

Mike Murdoch, a well-known Christian author, preacher and song writer, has this favorite saying: "Every problem a man will ever face in life is a wisdom problem."

This saying is based on the argument that a problem will not remain a problem as long as you have the wisdom to resolve it.

There is wisdom available for your peculiar circumstance keeping you stuck. You just need to become hungry enough to search for the wisdom to get out. I pray that what I have to share in this book, starting from the next chapter, will provide you with the wisdom you need to get out of "The Rat Race" and into "The God Race."

There Is Always A Way

Going back to 1 Corinthians 10:13, by far the best part of the thirteenth verse is the last part stating, *"...with every temptation (trial or adversity), God has made a way of escape."* Please understand, Paul was a man whom suffereed many trials and tribulations in his time. Here is a little glimpse of his resume:

"Are they servants of Christ? (I am out of my mind to talk like this.) I am more. I have worked much harder, been in prison more frequently, been flogged more severely, and been exposed to death again and again. 24 Five times I received from the Jews the forty lashes minus one. 25 Three times I was beaten with rods, once I was pelted with stones, three times I was shipwrecked, I spent a night and a day in the open sea,

" ²⁶ I have been constantly on the move. I have been in danger from rivers, in danger from bandits, in danger from my fellow Jews, in danger from Gentiles; in danger in the city, in danger in the country, in danger at sea; and in danger from false believers. ²⁷ I have labored and toiled and have often gone without sleep; I have known hunger and thirst and have often gone without food; I have been cold and naked. ²⁸ Besides everything else, I face daily the pressure of my concern for all the churches."

2 Corinthians 11:23-28 (NIV)

When you really consider the type of trials Paul faced, it is remarkable he would still write that God is faithful to always make a way of escape for you. You have to conclude he must have known what he was talking about.

Personally, I too have experienced some tough challenges in which I was convinced might wipe me out. Looking back today, I can agree with the apostle Paul that God truly has a way of escape amidst every trial. There is always a way out no matter how tough it looks.

Ancient Devils & Ancient Landmarks

As I mentioned earlier, a wise thing to do when you encounter a difficult trial is to ask yourself the question,

42

"Has anybody else ever been through what I am going through?" A good place to search for the answer to this question is the bible. Learn to search the scriptures for examples of challenges similar to the one you are facing. Study the character involved and what this character did to get out of trouble.

I remember, in the year 2008, when we started experiencing new adverse economic conditions in the United States. What started with the collapse of the mortgage/finance industry quickly cascaded down to affect so many other sectors of the economy. Soon after, everyone started to feel it's impact. The state of the credit industry caused many companies to fail and unemployment went through the roof. Many became afraid of personal finanacial adversity and started making wrong financial decisions in their panic response.

During one of my prayer times, I heard the spirit of the Lord ask me to go study the scriptures that chronicled the occassions when people experienced economic hardship. I studied to discover the reason for the economic adversity, the people it affected, the people that thrived in the middle of it and why they thrived. I started studying in Genesis about the first three famines that affected God's people. I discovered many divine laws and principles which helped those who thrived in those famines. I realized those laws and principles were still valid for the economic challenges we started to face in 2008 and I decided to apply them. The following year (2009) ended up becoming one of my best years financially. I was experiencing increase while many in the nation were experiencing their worst drought. I ended up preaching a series of messages to the congregation I pastored titled, "How to Prosper Financially in Hard Times." This also helped many of them turn their finances around.

It was at this time I learned that if you can find the ancient landmarks, you can discover ancient devils and how to take them out. The devil has no new tricks to cause adversity in your life. Many before you have found their way out of *the rat race* and you can too. I truly pray you do. Hence, I encourage you to pay close attention to the truths you are about to read in the next chapter.

Prayer:

Father, in the Name of Jesus, I ask you for wisdom: wisdom for living, building, my family relationships, my marriage, finances, my career, ministry, and wisdom to be who You have called me to be. Lord put within me a fresh hunger and a thirst for godly knowledge and wisdom. My God, I receive wisdom to get out of the rat race in Jesus Name. Amen!

Chapter 4

THE WAY OUT

"And though the Lord gives you the bread of adversity and the water of affliction, Yet your teachers will not be moved into a corner anymore; But your eyes shall see your teachers. [21] Your ears shall hear a word behind you, saying, "This is the way, walk in it," Whenever you turn to the right hand Or whenever you turn to the left.

Isaiah 30:20-21 *(NKJV)*

Success Roads Are Narrow

What does it mean to be out of *the rat race*? When are you out? While I was doing my research, I read several people's opinions of what it meant to them to be out of *the rat race*. Some said it meant moving away from the work place and working from home. They felt no longer in *the rat race* because they didn't have to get up and jump on the train or drive on the freeway to get to work anymore.

Really? Others expressed that retirement or no longer needing or having to work took them out of *the rat race*. Another said to get out of *the rat race* meant leaving a high pressured job and to take a simple position for work.

A few years ago, I was doing some consulting in Portland, Oregon and met a lady who was a systems developer. She was doing quite well financially, but then her contract ended. She called me one day and said she didn't want to be involved in *the rat race* of corporate America anymore and decided to take an administrative position in a hospital. She sounded like she believed this decision would get her out of the hustle and bustle. I had to tell her that more than likely she would dig herself a deeper hole and may never have a chance of getting free.

After spending some time talking with this lady, I realized her passion was writing poetry and in fact had written some beautiful poems. I looked at this lady and knew she could go far with her talent if she could just launch herself out from where she was to a platform where the world could see, appreciate, and celebrate her poetry. I began to encourage her. I told her if she could get her works published and known, she could get herself out of *the rat race*. Since our conversations, she has started to collect her poems. She is planning to publish a book of poetry in the near future.

Getting out of *the rat race* is not about moving from a big city to a small rural area nor is it about walking to work. Leaving a job so you don't have to work long hours does not get you out. In financial terms, you get out of *the rat race* by becoming financially independent from an employer.

When you get to a stage where you wake up in the morning and say you don't have to be anywhere by someone else's demand and your family is well taken care of – then it must mean you are out. When your monthly income is not from a job or jobs, but from investments you have built up, assets, residual income, and royalties from talents or gifts in your life – you are out. When what comes in on a monthly basis is more than what you need to maintain your life and family's monthly needs – you are out. If it takes $3,000 to take care of all your needs in a month and you make $3,200 from investments, assets, residual income, etc. – you're out!

Now that I have discussed what *the rat race* is, I want to share with you seven points on the subject of "How to get out of The Rat Race." I am very confident that if you follow these seven steps you *will* get out. The Spirit of the Lord reminded me of how He got my wife and me out of the financial *rat race* when we lived in England, and how He brought us to the USA where we are fulfilling our purpose and destiny today. What we are doing now is no longer in *The Rat Race* but in *The God Race*.

I am now going to share with you my experience and the things I know work. If you will make an effort to do these things, you also can be out of *the rat race*. For a Christian, this is serious stuff because we are in the last days. You no longer have ten or twenty years for God to help you get your act together. He needs you to get it together right now!

Many of you reading this have gifts and anointing to start impacting your world for Christ. You have been in church for quite some time, heard many sermons and are now filled with the word of God. God needs you. He can't afford for you to be trapped in *the rat race* any longer.

I read a book once where the author made this statement: "It is the responsibility of the church to get God's people out of any kind of bondage." I took this to heart. Debt is bondage! *The Rat Race* is bondage! I am also aware that the road to successfully getting out of the maze is a narrow one. Otherwise, many would have found it and used it. Here are some practical steps I have discovered over the years which will help you navigate your way out of the maze.

Get Out Of Debt

Step One: <u>Most important, get out of debt!</u>

No matter how we like to look at our situation, whoever you owe money to, you are that person's servant.

"The rich rules over the poor, and the borrower is a servant to the lender."   Proverbs 22:7 (NKJV)

The company holding the note on your car is the one you are serving when you go to the office. Your mortgage lenders, they are the ones you are serving. The financial debt system, the mammon system, becomes what you are serving.

Many Christians today easily choose to forego church meetings that conflict with their work schedules because they cannot afford to miss any opportunity to earn money. I don't say this to make anyone feel guilty or make you think it's an evil thing to do. We have to face the reality of it.

For many saints, it's easier to call the Pastor and say "I'm sorry I can't make it, I have to work," than it is to call the boss and say, "I have a special prayer meeting and I can't make it to work." The boss is going to say, "Prayer what? What's a prayer meeting got to do with your work?

You better be here or you are out of a job!" This is why in Deuteronomy 28:13 it says God's desire is that we, *"shall be the head and not the tail "* and in Deuteronomy 28:12, *" to be lenders to nations and not borrowers"*. Why? Because Solomon told us in Proverbs 22:7 that as long as you are a borrower you are a servant to the lender.

I remember a time when I had already started my journey in full time ministry but had to go back into the corporate world to work as an Information technology consultant on the side. I did this not because I wanted to do the extra work, but because I needed to. I had to make sure my family's needs were met and that we didn't lose our home. I also had made some foolish financial decisions which created unwanted debt to pay off. Please understand that it is easy to get back into *the rat race* (after getting out) because of foolish financial decisions.

Know you are a servant to mammon until you get out of debt. Resist all temptations to finance anything from now on. Only borrow with wisdom for capital investments on income generating assets. The only time borrowing makes sense is when you are buying an asset. Not for a liability. Learn the clear distinctions of what an asset is versus what a liability is.

An asset will bring money to you and a liability will take money away from you. For an example, which may shock you, your home you live in is not an asset, it is a liability. Your house takes money from your pocket every month. You make payments, you pay insurance, you spend money to fix things and make it look nice with landscaping, etc. It continually takes money from you. The only real estate property that is an asset is the one you don't live in. It's the one in which someone else is paying the mortgage for you. That is the only true real estate asset.

A good example of wise borrowing is found in the story about the widow in II Kings chapter 4. Elisha told the widow to borrow vessels from her neighbors and in return she would receive the asset of oil to meet her and her son's needs. It was the type of borrowing that would generate return.

There is a term used today with regards to wise borrowing. It is the term "OPM" - Other People's Money. The wealthy people of our world have mastered the art of using other people's money to make money – such as banks. The banks don't have any money of their own. The money they have to work with is our money. They invite us to put our money in their bank for a 2% return on our savings and then turn around and lend us back that money on our credit cards at 13% interest and tell us it is a special deal. Then, when you miss your payment, they hike it up to

19%. If you are not vigilant, they send you a letter with small print telling you they hiked it up to 24%.

I consider banks and financial systems to be the wisest institutions I know of in this mammon system. They know how to use other people's money for their own profit. They beg you to use their credit cards with the hope you won't be able to honor the payments. They don't want you to make your payments. If you make your payments regularly and you begin to pay it down, they start sending you checks and enticing you to borrow more. They don't like it when you make your payments.

This credit system is designed for those who are not going to make their payments. They are waiting for that unfortunate day so they can send you a letter with a thirty-five dollar charge. Have you noticed on your department store cards that if you are making your payments they send you all kinds of offers and catalogs trying to make you spend more unnecessarily? Then when you can't make the payment, all of a sudden they are not so nice to you anymore. They send you nasty letters and start calling you at all hours of the day. So the first thing you must do to get out of this *rat race* is to get out of debt.

Live Within Your Means

Step Two: <u>Lower your cost of living to the bare minimum</u>.

In Luke 14:28-29, Jesus makes a statement: *"For which of you, intending to build a tower does not sit down first and count the cost, whether he has enough money to finish it – lest after he has laid the foundation, and is not able to finish, all who see it begin to mock him."*

In essence, Jesus is saying you need a financial plan and a budget. You need to have a budget for every project in your life.

Anyone who has been in financial trouble will tell you it happened because they did not have a budget. The easiest way to lose sight of your expenditures is to have no budget. A person who has no budget will go to the mall and if they like what they see, they just buy "it." You don't know when you don't have the money to spend because you have no budget. You have nothing written down to show you where you're at with what money you have. When you get a paycheck, a wise Christian first separates their tithes pulling aside a percentage for savings and then lives on the portion leftover. This is why it is important to know what you have left. Most people will tell you what they bring in is not enough to meet their needs. Let's be honest with ourselves, they only say that because they are living beyond their means.

I am one of five children in our family. The first four of us are males. We were often mad at our father because he set a financial standard for handling money that was just too hard for us. Our dad started his working career by saving 60% of his income and living only on the 40% remaining. Then when he started having children, he switched spending 60% of it and saving 40%. I used to wonder how he managed to do that.

I remember as a young kid, my parents had an argument concerning moving to a more expensive part of the city. He would say, "No, we are not spending money for that." He lived like that because all his life he was a wage earner; he was not a business man. He had learned to discipline himself to live within a certain percentage of his income. Do you know what that means? It means he had to give up some things. It meant he had to sacrifice.

There is a good side to this. I was telling some men at breakfast the other day that my father put all five of his children through college and not one of us took out a student loan. How did he pay for that? He was a salary earner with a monthly paycheck. He must have sacrificed a lot to do so. He must have given up many things he could have enjoyed in order to put away the savings.

I remember my Pastor used to say to us, when he was teaching on biblical economies, "delayed gratification is a sign of maturity." My Pastor would also say that you were immature if you were in the habit of spending money to buy whatever you felt like having. He cautioned us that we didn't have to buy everything we could afford to buy. He taught us how to stop and ask the question, "do I absolutely need this?" – Most of the time the answer was, "no."

I am acquainted with a retired financial adviser in his seventies. He is very financially blessed. He still takes a pencil and notepad around every day to record his financial transactions. When he buys something, he takes his notepad and writes it down. After years of running a very successful business and several years into his retirement, he still uses a budget. He sold his business for millions and he is totally debt free. He owes nothing on his homes or cars, yet he still practices using a budget that made him successful in the first place.

I would like to suggest that you take the time right now to make a list of what you spend money on monthly. Critically go through the list and ask yourself what you could take out of the list – something you really should not be spending money on. Ask yourself, "Would it kill me? Will I die if I don't spend on a particular item?"

I remember some years ago how my children cried and complained when I told my wife that Dish TV network had to go. My son was sure he could not live without the NFL channels. I replaced Dish TV with the Sky Angel Network - fifteen dollars a month! I told my son that when Myles spent too much time watching TV as a boy his mother told him, "If you keep watching all that TV you will never be on TV!"

Today Myles Monroe is a popular Christian preacher, teacher, author of bestseller books and he is frequently featured on television programs. His mother knew he had a destiny to fulfill. So when my children complained about getting rid of Dish TV I paid no attention because I asked myself, "Will anyone die over the loss of that network? No! It has to go." I had to make sure our household could operate in the black on a pastor's allowance.

When I was consulting on the side, I was able to financially bring in four times more than needed to run my household and monthly expenses. Plus, I was able to invest three quarters of it. I am letting you in on the principle that worked for me. When the Lord started this process of getting out of *the rat race* for us, we fought to get out of debt first. I mean we literally fought! My wife and I had different ideas as to what we could and should afford. Many times she would be very upset with me. But I knew I had to stand my ground. I became head strong on getting out of debt. There was no doubt this was the direction the Lord wanted us to take.

Soon, we were out of debt. I then moved to the next step of cutting down the budget. As I mentioned earlier, I made a list and took out what was not absolutely necessary. I then began step three in my process to get out of *the rat race*.

Maximize Your Income

Step Three: Increasing your income.

I started to look for ways to increase my income to the max. Step two usually helps you to realize how much you need in step three. Step two is where you find out you do not have enough income to continue your plan of getting out of the maze. It is in step two that you find there is nothing more to cut, and even though you are out of debt, you need to have extra income to save as well as invest.

This process started for me in 1997. When my son was born, I cut my budget to the barest minimum and found I still did not have enough income. I started to ask the Lord, "What can I do to help this situation?" The answer came as a door opened for me to shift into a different career path. This was prior to becoming a full-time pastor.

My earned my academic degree in Chemical Engineering. However, I forced myself to return to school to learn about Information Technology. At that time, computer technicians, programmers and consultants were in high demand, and were making very good money because of that demand. I learned this form friends and family working in the information technology industry and I saw how much money they were making. I decided that was what I wanted to do to increase my income.

As I began to work in my new career, I soon made more than what I needed. We continued living on the budget we had figured out earlier. This gave me excess to save and invest. You need to do the same.

You must look at the job you do today and figure out how you can bring yourself to the highest income level while still living on a bare bones budget. Most people make the mistake of thinking because they make more they must spend more. You must check all your options. Can you work your way up at your present job and make more? Can you further educate yourself and move to another career? What can you do?

No matter where you are right now, you can start doing something. Do not get discouraged if this seems too hard to achieve; continue with me and I will help you to see that I am still going somewhere with this. I have yet to get to the reasons for which you need to move into this position. I have not mentioned anything about passion and direction for your life. So after digesting these first three steps, let's move on.

I knew that Information Technology was not my destiny. It was just a means toward my destiny. At the time, I did not know what my destiny was supposed to be. I just knew at information technology. I was very good at learning new things and I wanted to take advantage of that to get myself out of *the rat race*. After making the move and increasing my salary, it was time to move on to Step Four.

Invest the Difference

Step Four: <u>Invest the difference between your income and expenditures</u>.

What do I mean by invest the difference? If I make $3,000 a month and I need $2,200 to take care of our household needs, I will have $800 extra. Don't run out to buy new shoes, new dresses or go on a vacation. Don't tell yourself you have a windfall of extra money. Invest that money. Remember, you are trying to get out of *the rat race*. In order to get out of *the rat race* you must have some kind of returns coming in from investments. It's called "making your money work for you."

Take that difference and make it work for you. Eventually, this frees you from having to work for an income for the rest of your life. Some people might say, "But, Pastor, I don't have any money to invest." Understand that you have to start somewhere, no matter how small. Even if you can find a small bond somewhere that has compounded interest and you only put away $50 a month. You will eventually increase that to $100 a month and so on as your income level increases.

Open up a gold account. Look for investment property. I am not trying to give you financial advice as to where to invest your money, that's not my subject or assignment for this time, just invest somewhere after studying your options. Get all the information that's right for you, and study it in order to invest wisely.

In the Bible Jesus tells a story teaching the profound principle of money stewardship. "*For the kingdom of heaven is as like a man traveling to a far country, who called his own servants and delivered his goods to them. And to one he gave five talents, to another two, and to another one, to each according to his own ability; and immediately he went on a journey. Then he who had received the five talents went and traded with them, and made another five talents. And like wise he who had received two gained two more also. But he who had received one went and dug in the ground and hid his lord's money. After a long time the lord of those servants came and settled accounts with them. So he who had received five talents came and brought five other talents, saying, 'Lord, you delivered to me five talents; look, I have gained five more talents besides them.' His lord said to him, 'Well done, good and faithful servant; you were faithful over a few things, I will make you ruler over many things. Enter into the joy of your lord.' He also who had received two talents came and said, 'Lord, you delivered to me two talents; look, I have gained two more talents besides them.' His lord said to him, 'Well done, good and faithful servant; you have been faithful over a few things, I will make you ruler over many things. Enter into the joy of your lord.' Then he who had received the one talent came and said, 'Lord, I knew you to be a hard man, reaping where you have not sown, and gathering where you have not scattered seed. And I was afraid, and went and hid your talent in the ground. Look, there you have what is yours.' But his lord answered and said to him, 'You wicked and lazy servant, you knew that I reap where I have not sown, and gather where I have not scattered seed. So you ought to have deposited my money with the bankers, and at my coming I would have received back my own with interest. So take the talent from him, and give it to him who has ten talents. For to everyone who has, more will be given, and he will have abundance; but from him who does not have, even what he has will be taken away. And cast the unprofitable servant into the outer darkness. There will be weeping and gnashing of teeth."*

Matt. 25:14-30 *(NKJV)*

Notice how Jesus said to give the one talent to the one who had ten? Then he said "to everyone who *has*, more will be given." *Has* what? The ability to multiply and retain what has been give to them. Those who do not, even what they have will be taken away from them. Why? What is He talking about? He is talking about our spiritual ability. He uses this real life parable to get his message across. He uses a financial lesson to get across a spiritual precept. It's a big lesson for Christians. Christians must become financially savvy.

When we read a story given to us from the Lord, it should wet our appetites to learn more. It should make us want to educate ourselves better on the subject by reading more books about financial wisdom. These financial lessons are not taught in elementary school, Junior High, or High School. Unless you're taking special elected financial classes, it's not taught in College either. Being well educated with degrees does not mean you are going to be wise financially. If it were so, there would be less broke College Professors driving old, worn out cars.

We have all heard stories of people who have made lots of money, yet ended up bankrupt. A good example is a former world heavyweight boxing champion who made several millions of dollars with his talent during his earlier life time and lost it all. Why? He lost it all because he lacked financial intelligence and guidance. Many who have received windfalls of money, such as lotteries worth millions, became broke soon after because they were never taught any wisdom in financial principles.

To sum up Step Four, we must invest our excess difference of income, much like the example in the story of the talents told by Jesus in Matthew 25, and expect a return. We must be good and faithful servants with our income.

Prayer:

Father, in the Name of Jesus, I ask you to forgive me for not being a better steward of my finances. I make up my mind today to make the necessary changes. Please grant me wisdom to know how to use budgets to spend carefully, how to make more money and how to wisely invest the money I have after paying my bills. Father, I thank you for the wisdom and grace to get out of the rat race in Jesus Name. Amen!

The purpose
of **life** is to
discover your **gift.**
The **work** of life is
to **develop** it.
The meaning
of life is to
give your
gift away

Chapter 5

ENTERING THE GOD RACE

These last three steps are the most important steps to getting out of *the rat race*. You must follow through on these steps so you can find a life of purpose while at the same time, do well financially. These three steps are going to show you how to get out of "just" working a job to making a life of using your gifts and talents. If you follow them, it will get you from hating what you do, to doing what you love. This is how you enter your "God Race."

Discover Your Gifts & Calling

Step Five: <u>Discover your predominant gift and life calling</u>.

If you have ever been in my congregation for more than two months, you would have heard me talk about these subjects. Helping God's children to discover and walk into their God ordained purpose is, I believe, the predominant call of God on my life. I am truly passionate about it. In my opinion, the five most important questions concerning your life are: Who are you? Where did you come from? Why are you here? What can you do? Where are you going when you die? Whatever you do make sure in your lifetime to get the answer to all of these questions.

The saints that attend the church I pastor have heard me preach on the importance of discovering your predominant gift and calling. It helps to answer the question "Why am I here?" As a matter of fact, most of the people under my mentorship are in transition from knowing who they are to developing themselves into being ready for deployment. These people also know their personal passion. They may not know how to fully utilize their gifts yet or be at a place where they are excellent at executing their calling, but at least they know who they are.

I urge you to begin to seek the face of the Almighty God for what gifts and calling you has been given. Everybody has been given unique gifts and talents. You need to get close to the Lord and ask Him questions. Who am I? What is my predominant gift? Who am I suppose to be?"

The Bible says it very clearly in Jeremiah 33:3, *"Call to Me, and I will answer you, and show you great and mighty things, which you do not know."* If you ask God, He will tell you. I am not talking about asking Him in a thirty second prayer and then five minutes later saying, "He hasn't told me anything!" I am talking about a life where you are continuously seeking the face of God as you are growing in relationship with Him. In your prayer time you must tell Him, "Lord I surrender my life to You" and ask Him, "Lord reveal to me who You have made me to be. Show me Your plan and purpose for my life." It will be just a matter of time and you will know the answers to your questions.

Men walking with God were not just employees working jobs for living. If you notice, from Genesis to Revelation most Bible characters walking with God were entrepreneurs and ministers. Even Jesus could not use low level employees on his ministry team. Read the Gospels and study all twelve apostles.

I know we have all heard these sermons telling us that Jesus picked these low lives, good-for-nothing people to follow him. In light of the culture at that time Peter and Andrew were businessmen. When Jesus said, "follow me," they could follow Him. Also, James and John were businessmen. One of the Gospels tells us that when Jesus called James and John, they left what they had to their servants and father to run the fishing business. Do not read some of these things with religious eye glasses!

If Matthew was not a big shot in the tax collection office (our version of the IRS office) at that time, he would not have been able to influence other tax collectors to go to his home for a dinner party with Jesus. The Bible tells us that Jesus went to where Matthew worked and said, "Come follow me." Jesus had a better plan for him. Just a few scriptures later it tells us about the dinner at Matthew's house. All of his fellow tax collectors came and Jesus ministered to them at Matthew's house. I submit to you that Matthew could not have been the office janitor.

In addition, Luke the apostle, was a physician. Physicians were highly respected at that time just as they are today. You must see why Jesus was able to pick these men. He could not afford to pick anyone who would say, "I am sorry, but my credit cards are maxed out. Plus, I have to work at my job for my boss who pays my wages. Therefore, I cannot follow you." That was not the story for any of the guys that worked for Jesus.

God is looking for men willing to work for Him, not just for money. You have heard this scripture before: *"Many are called, but few are chosen."* Every child of God is called. You will hear people say that a person has a "special calling" on their life as if only an appointed few have callings. That is not true. Everyone has been called yet not everyone is available. If you are not available you cannot be chosen! The Lord dropped that into my spirit one night during prayer – people are not available for Him to use.

God has a plan for your life, but if you are too busy slaving for the dollar everyday than you are stuck in this *rat race* and He can't really do much with you. It's because you're not available.

At church when it's announced that it's time to do some community outreach, you always say, "Sorry, I can't go. I have to work." When a special prayer meeting is called, the first thing we have to consider is if this is going to interfere with my hours of work. We let our job dictate whether or not we are allowed to go to a prayer meeting.

Please understand me, working for God does not mean you have to be in the clergy. It does not mean that you have to be a pastor or a preacher. That is not what I mean. Working for God means that you get to a place where what you do is for Kingdom purposes. It's for Kingdom advancement rather than just making money to be able to pay bills.

To clearly drive home the point of the last three steps, I want to go through a story in the Bible about a man named Jacob. Jacob's story clearly depicts many of the points I've made. The Holy Spirit led me to a discovery in the word I had never seen before.

Do you remember Jacob? He was that smart guy who made a nice meal and stole his brother's birthright. Then he out-smarted him again by getting the blessing from their father. In actuality, Jacob's actions ended up being a lot of smart efforts for nothing because it was already ordained that he would have the birthright and the blessing. God had already told his mother while he was still in the womb that Jacob was the one to get the blessing. It could not have gone the other way because then it would have been against the will of God.

God had a better way but Jacob took things into his own hands and defrauded his brother who became very angry with him. Jacob knew that as soon as his father died, his brother would want to kill him. So he decided to leave. His mother encouraged him to get away and go to her brother Laban's house.

On Jacob's journey to his uncle's house, he stopped along the way and made a vow to God. He told God that if He kept him safe during this time, he would come back to the same spot and give God a tithe of everything God would bless him with. When Jacob got to the city where his Uncle lived, he stopped at a well to water his animals and asked for some information. Let's read the following verses to see what happened next. I want you to clearly understand the point I'm making in Step five.

"And Jacob said to them, 'My brethren where are you from?' And they said, 'We are from Haran.' Then he said to them, 'Do you know Laban, the son of Nahor?' And they said, 'We know him.' So he said to them, 'Is he well?' And they said, 'He is well. And look, his daughter Rachel is coming with the sheep.' Then he said, 'Look, it is still high day; it is not time for the cattle to be gathered together. Water the sheep, and go and feed them.' "
Genesis 29:4-7 *(NKJV)*

I want you to pay attention to that last verse. There's something I never noticed before. The Lord showed me that Jacob's gift was raising animals. As soon as he shows up in a new area he notices that the men there were about to make a mistake with their animals.

Instantly, Jacob starts to use his gift with his knowledge about animals. He tells the guys, "No, no, this is not the time to do this." He tells them it's the high time of the day, not the time to gather the cattle together yet. His skills concerning animals showed up in him.

Then Rachel comes on the scene and he takes one look at her and says, "Wow", that's my uncle's daughter? She's beautiful!" When he gets to his uncle's house, he tells him he has a skill to offer him. It's an ability to look after animals. Laban is happy with the idea and offers him a position to take care of his sheep. In verse 15, Laban asked Jacob what he thought his wages should be.

We must realize that when we work, we exchange our ability for money. So, if we exchange our ability for money, we should bring forth our best gift – our most lucrative gift. For example, let's say you have a gift for sewing or hairstyling, but you are also very good and gifted with numbers. Hairstyling brings in $50 per hour however becoming an accountant brings in $100 per hour. Which should you do? If you are going to exchange your gift for money, you might as well exchange your gift for the most money you can make.

So Jacob puts his best foot forward and offers his best gift to Laban. Now when his uncle asks what his wages should be, Jacob says in verses 16 and 17: "*Now Laban had two daughters: the name of the elder was Leah and the name of the younger was Rachel. Leah's eyes were delicate, but Rachel was beautiful in form and appearance.*" The bible was telling us in a nice way that Leah was not as beautiful as Rachel. In verse 18, "*Now Jacob loved Rachel; so he said, 'I will serve you seven years for Rachel your younger daughter.'*"

So Jacob and Laban made the employment deal. The deal was that Jacob would bring his gift to serve Laban in exchange for his daughter. Jacob was good with raising animals (his gift) and in exchange he would receive a paycheck: Laban's daughter. It sounds good but Jacob got himself into a kind of a *rat race* because he was now bound for seven years.

Sometimes, I wish we could turn back the clocks to where men had to work seven years for their brides. Perhaps that would fix the problem of spousal abuse. By the time one labored for seven years to get his bride, that person would truly appreciate her; she would be a most precious gift! Jacob's gift made room for him in Laban's house. Remember in Proverbs 18:16 it says, *"A man's gift makes room for him, and brings him before great men."*

Jacob's story goes on to tell us that as a result of Jacob's gift, Laban was blessed for his animal material wealth started to increase. It is the same when we take our gift to our employer. We help the employer become successful in their business. The employer makes money from our gifts and in return gives us a fraction of their increase for our service. This is why I have come to the conclusion that employment is not God's best blessings for us. Entrepreneurship is God's best.

When you own your own business, you maximize your own gift and receive in return your best reward. When you work for someone else, they are the one deciding what fraction of the revenue you will get back for your talents and gifts. Please know, I am not asking you to immediately quit your job. First there are steps and ground work needed to accomplish the goal.

Tiger Woods gets paid a lot of money doing what he enjoys. Michael Jordan received a huge amount of money doing what he enjoyed. Bill Gates has become one of the richest men in the world doing what he loves. Most people don't know this about Mr. Gates, but, he did not achieve his success because he was looking for money. He was passionate about technology. He had a dream about making this technology available to every household. Donald Trump loves what he does.

It's not so much the money that men like these go after; it's for the love of the game of real estate. They have a talent for investment and they love doing it. They sleep and dream about these things all the time. It's their passion!

You may ask, "Are you trying to tell me my dreams and passions could get me out of *the rat race*?" Yes, that is what I'm trying to tell you and oh yes they can! Because what you have a passion for will bring out the best in you. And the best in you will eventually bring you out of obscurity and into the lime light. You will get to the place where people will pay you money to enjoy the fruits of your talent and gifts.

The people in Hollywood use their gift of acting to go before the cameras creating movies we later pay money at theaters to watch in order to enjoy their gifts and talents in action. Every time you purchase a cinema ticket, you are making those involved with the making of the film wealthy because of their talents and gifts.

One man's gift was to write books. He was a pastor named Tommy Tenney. He wrote the book "One Night with the King." One day, CBN came to him and said they wanted to make a movie of his book. He signed a contract with CBN to receive royalties if the movie should make any money. When "One Night with the King" came into the theaters, it made millions. Guess what? Tommy Tenney made millions also. Now and forever, anytime that movie is shown or the DVD is sold, he gets a check. He made millions doing what he loves to do with a passion - writing books.

There is a preacher named Mike Murdoch who writes songs. He has probably written three or four thousand songs in his lifetime. It is his passion. But nobody knows him as a singer of the songs he writes. He doesn't sing for the world. He just loves writing them and people buy his songs to sing on their own records. He receives royalties for something he loves to do — write songs. What talents and gifts are you sleeping on? What will it take to bring them out of you?

Develop Your Gifts

Step Six: Start spending time and money on training and self development.

Do this in preparation from job to purpose. This step is the secret to the entire subject of getting out of *the rat race*. If you ever find yourself stuck in a job you don't like and you desire to get into what you really want to do, you must start training yourself.

You need to get into self-development classes on the subjects you are interested in. Prepare yourself to make the switch when the opportunity comes you way. It will do you no good to have great opportunities come across your path when you are not trained or prepared to take advantage of them.

Remember, people reward us financially for the problems we solve. Even if you clean floors at a big company, you are being paid for the problem they need solved. If singing is your gift and you have dreamed about singing all your life, and this is what you want to do; you must train your gift. You have to put in the time to prepare and develop your dream. Otherwise, no one will be interested in your gift. We don't pay money for a movie that has average actors in it. We wait to pay money for those who have developed their gifts.

One of the reasons God's children have felt they have nothing to offer is because they have not developed the gifts God has given them. Some have not discovered it yet. Some have discovered their gifts and talk about it, but never do anything about it. They are not willing to pay the price to develop the gift.

I will use myself as an example. If I had not spent the time and money to develop myself in order to become a pastor and teacher, you would not have spent the money or the time to read this book. My congregation would not be sitting in my church each Sunday and Wednesday listening to what I have to teach. I was able to realize my dream. Because of this dream, I signed up for Bible school in Believer's College, where I found it useful to do eighteen months in Minister's training school.

Attending many hours of conferences and training seminars became a big part of my life. I did all this because I knew I had to increase my knowledge and wisdom so that I might have something to offer others. I knew that when I opened my mouth; I had to make sense to those who would be listening. In contrast, if my preparation and development was not completed, the first time I stood in front of a congregation, no matter how sincere my heart, those listening would probably have walked out before I finished!

What are your gifts? How far have you developed your gifts? Has anyone offered to exchange their money for your gifts? If we advertised your gift now, would anyone be interested in giving money for the level your gift is at now? Don't feel bad if no one is interested yet. It just means you have to start developing and training yourself. You see, the professional athletes I mentioned earlier signed large contracts with big companies. Do you think these big companies would have been interested in signing with an average athlete? No.

I remember when I wanted to get a particularly very expensive pair of shoes called "Air Jordan." The shoes were expensive because Michael Jordan's name was on them. He was at the top of his basketball career at the time. The manufacturers knew that using his name would sell those shoes at top dollar.

To those standing in line to buy them, it was as if those shoes were going to make you as good an athlete as Michael Jordan! People were willing to buy those shoes that cost six times more than another shoe that didn't have the brand name, even though the others had the same quality. It happened because somebody developed their gift by practicing three to five hours a day doing free throws. Michael Jordan developed his gift until he was one of the best in the world.

When are people going to exchange their money to enjoy your gift? Think hard about it. This is why I am saying you must spend time training and developing yourself so you can make the switch. Avoid working for just the money. Rather, work for the gain of wisdom, skill, and experience.

I was sharing with a man about this subject when he began to complain about the way the company he worked for was doing business. My advice to him was, "Do not, for one second, allow yourself to focus on what is right or wrong with the company. That is not your business. You are there to acquire skills. Be sure you acquire those skills, because the Lord is taking you somewhere after you learn them. Many times we do not understand that the skills we require must be learned in someone else's company for the day that the Lord sets us up in our own company. So when it gets tough, do not get out. When it is tough, find out how you can survive it. This is also training. When you have your own company and you come across these problems, you will know how to survive them to help your company become strong."

Did you notice in the story that Jacob became more skillful in his gift as he worked for Laban? Did you notice that it never mentioned that when he was living at home he was skillful with animals? The Bible says that while he was working with his uncle, the flocks increased. The herd was healthy and robust in reproducing their young. Laban finally realized that he was blessed abundantly because of Jacob and he decided he could not afford to let Jacob go from being his herdsman. Laban, the Bible says, "was conniving and crafty."

After the agreed upon seven years of labor in exchange for his daughter Rachel, Laban knew Jacob would leave him. So he came up with a plan that would make Jacob stay. On the wedding night, Laban tricked Jacob by giving him his other daughter Leah instead of his desired Rachel without him knowing. How does a man not know that the woman he consummates the marriage with is not the women he meant to marry? Now, that's another story I don't have time to get into.

However, the trick worked. Laban knew that the love Jacob had for Rachel would keep him working there another seven years. During those years, Jacob continued to build his skills while working for another man's business. The day finally came when Jacob was ready to make the trade of his labor for Rachel. He knew he had acquired the skills to get out of *the rat race*. He had the confidence to see he was good at what he did and he was ready to go out on his own.

Note that before you make a switch, make sure you have made a difference in the place where you work now before you start boasting about doing better on your own. You know you are using your gift to make a difference when managers and CEO's are noticing you. Then you are ready to step out and use the same gift to work for yourself.

In Genesis 30:26, Jacob goes to Laban and says: *"Give me my wives and my children for whom I have served you, and let me go; for you know my service which I have done for you. And Laban said to him, 'Please stay, if I have found favor in your eyes, for I have learned by experience that the Lord has blessed me for your sake.'"* Then he said, *"Name me your wages, and I will give it."*

Now you have to decide, what kind of worker are you? There are those who say, "I quit!" and the boss says, "Oh, thank-you very much! Good-bye." There are some workers who say they are quitting and the boss calls them in to the office and says "Please, what can I do to make you stay? Name your price. Do you want a pay raise? What do you want?" You have to figure out which category you belong to and why you are in that category. Once you do, it will determine if you are working your game, your gift, or whether you're just earning a salary.

Jacob came to the decision that he wanted to move away from being an employee. He knows he is good at what he does, so he answers Laban by telling him he wants his own stock. He makes a deal with Laban to keep every speckled and spotted sheep born from this time forward in order to start his own heard. Laban quickly agrees, knowing so few speckled or spotted sheep are born and they are usually the weaker ones. Laban figures he has the better part of the deal hoping to have Jacob for an employee for a long time.

With Jacob's developed skill and the anointing and blessing of God, the herd began to multiply with speckled and spotted sheep. They were proving to be the strongest and healthiest of the stock. Jacob raised a large herd for himself, surpassing Laban's. He then announced to Laban that it was time for him to separate from his employment with him. Laban realized Jacob had all the best sheep and he didn't want him to go. But Jacob got out of *the rat race*. His financial independence got him out. It got him from being an employee to a business owner. When he left Laban, he was running his own large herd.

When you read the beginning of the story, did you read that Jacob had anything of value when he showed up at Laban's? Did he have any animals of his own? No. He started with nothing. In fact, when Jacob left with his rightfully earned herd of animals, Laban's sons said he had stolen all of their father's glory. This word "glory" is translated from the Hebrew word "kabod" which means *"heaviness — full of weight and honor."* They were describing the amount of wealth Jacob was taking with him.

Maximize Your Potential

Step Seven: <u>Maximize your talent and gift to impact lives, while at the same time making an income and receiving residual income.</u>

Everyone falls into a different category. Some of you are working jobs and many of you know it is not what you really want to do for the rest of your life. Your heart is not in it.

Recently, a lady was telling me how she enjoyed her job. But lately, she began to realize it was not what she wanted to do with her life. What I noticed was that this lady had turned her life over to God and He was working up the passion inside of her. It had caused her to have a different vision about her life and she was beginning to see what God had for her future.

There are some people who know what they want to do, but are still at a low level of their game. They have not started to make the best of it yet. This is what step seven is all about.

If you study step seven closely, after finishing the previous steps, you will be on your way out of *the rat race*. By knowing the previous steps, you will understand that you don't get out of *the rat race* because your income increases, you get out by following all of the steps that I have discussed:

1. Get out of debt,

2. Discipline yourself to lowering your cost of living,

 3. Increase your income,

4. Save and invest all you can

5. Find what your gift/talent is

6. Train and build your talent

I was counseling a long-time friend and fellow co-worker about his financial situation. It was obvious that his issue was not that he didn't make enough money. In 2007, my wife and I flew across the country to visit with him and his family. At that time his base salary was $140,000 a year.

I knew, as a friend, I had to tell it to him straight that there was no excuse for him not to be able to afford a living on his salary. I told him it had nothing to do with the amount of money he was making. It was simply because he was undisciplined with his money budget. I know so many people who would do very well with even half his salary.

You cannot have the mindset that when you get that bigger salary, everything is going to be fine. Without these seven steps, you will end up in a financial mess, no matter how much money you make or receive in a lump sum. Remember, we talked about how many lottery winners are totally broke within a few years of their winning. To do well financially, you must use the combination of these seven steps. I'll repeat number seven again: *Maximize your gifts and talents to impact **other** people's lives while making regular income and receiving residual income.*

Here's a list of five ways people can generate income. Notice the first four regard how to increase your finances. But if you don't know how to use number five, you will still not get out of *the rat race.*

5 Ways To Generate Income:

- Salary or commissions.
- Own a small or medium size business. *Usually at this level you are still personally involved with the daily affairs of the business.*
- Own a large business. *At this level, daily business activities are conducted by paid employees not the owner.*
- Receive honorariums or royalties. *This is common for speakers, authors and singers.* Royalties can become residual

income for life; which I believe is one of God's best for you.

- Make money through investments.

Back to our example of the heavy boxing champion whom I talked about earlier. He ended up broke after making millions because he did not know how to practice sound investing. Make sure that when you apply what I have been teaching you, that you put making sound investments, with your money, the top priority.

You must teach yourself the principles of how to invest your money. These things have not been taught in school, so more than likely, you have not learned even the basic principles of how to manage investments. You need to buy books, magazines and CD's on financial principles of investing. Gain some wisdom from those who have already been successful. There are plenty of successful Christians that have written books and produce a number of CD's with helpful information. Learn to make your money work for you.

When I go to *Barnes & Noble* book store, I can tell a lot about people without even knowing them just by the section of books they choose. When you see people spending time in the business section of the magazines with titles like "Business Weekly" or "Fortune Magazine," you know those people are serious about learning all they can to make their money work for them. Some guys are looking through all the car magazines and the motorcycle magazines, but are not able to buy the Harley they have always dreamed about owning. They must continue to dream because they never took the time to educate themselves to learn about how to manage money in order to someday enjoy those things.

In order to get to this investment level you must become skillful and diligent in what you do. It is easier to become diligent in what you are passionate about, hence the need to switch from a basic job level to a job fulfilling your passion. My pastor use to say that, "JOB" meant "Just Over Broke." He said, "as long as you work a job, you will always be Just Over the Broke level."

It's time to stop doing what you hate. I want to repeat that. For Christians who know the time is short, it is time you stop doing what you hate! I challenge you to take this year as the year you will start developing yourself into what you want to do following your passion.

Many people have asked me what I thought this year would bring. I tell them from my heart that this is a year for development; my own development and the development of my congregation.

You personally are the one who should determine the amount of income you will comprise. My passion is to preach the gospel but my income is not limited by my passion to preach. Even if I don't receive an income I will continue to preach. I have developed myself with enough skills to be called to speak and receive honorariums. I can also make money through my books, message CDs and DVDs, as well as for conducting leadership training sessions which is another one of my passions. I am glad for this season of my life when I am financially free to follow my passion: preaching and impacting other people's lives.

You determine the amount of income you can make by the value you add to yourself. It's time to make up your mind. Start writing your goals for this year. It doesn't matter if it is the beginning of the year, the middle, or the end. Write your goals down now. Write down what value you are going to add to yourself this year. Make a plan of how you are going to take yourself to a higher level where people are willing to reward you.

"A man's gift makes room for him, And brings him before great men."
Proverbs 18:16 (NKJV)

"Do you see a man diligent and skillful in his business? He will stand before kings; he will not stand before obscure men."
Proverbs 22:29 (AMP)

Those who get to show off their skills before kings and great men are usually on top of their game. Here, I am not talking about average. You cannot be an average artist or athlete and end up in front of a king or in front of the president of your country. You would have to be one of the best. That is what the Bible is trying to say in this passage of Proverbs. For you to stand in front of important people, you must be skillful in what you do.

When I was younger, I lived in England for many years. At the time, every year the Queen of England would honor and give awards to the best athlete, artist or music entertainer in the country. These were people being recognized in their field as "excellent." Sometimes the Queen would make someone a "Sir" or "Knight" depending on their accomplishments in life.

The story of Jacob reveals that he eventually stood before a king later in his life. When his son Joseph brought his family to Egypt, Jacob not only stood before the king, but the Bible tells us he "blessed" the king. It says the king came to Jacob and said, "Bless me." Can you imagine the king kneeling before Jacob asking to be blessed by him? Can you get to a level where you not only stand before a king on earth but you bless a king? It is possible if you are following your passion.

In Nigeria during annual church conferences, the kings of many tribal areas come and sit in the front row. They come because these ministers operate in an excellent level. What is your field? Can you get to a level where you can fulfill your purpose and destiny in life? Can you get to a place where you can stand up before the King of Kings and the Lord of Lords?

What I have placed before you is not the wisdom of Daniel Mateola. It is the wisdom of God on these matters. God is interested in you! He is telling us, "Time is short. I put gifts and talents in my people. They cannot use them because they are stuck in menial jobs and are not using their gifts for the destinies I have for them."

Start today. If you do, your life will never be the same again.

Prayer:

Father, I thank you for physical and emotional strength, and for health and wisdom to excel in my work. I ask for the special grace to develop my gifts and talents to a high level so that I may stand before kings and not mere men. Please help me to overcome every obstacle that could stop me from getting to the top of my field. I ask all of this in the matchless name of Jesus Christ of Nazareth. Amen!

Chapter 6

STEPPING OFF THE BLOCKS

"24 Do you not know that those who run in a race all run, but one receives the prize? Run in such a way that you may obtain it. 25 And everyone who competes for the prize is temperate in all things. Now they do it to obtain a perishable crown, but we for an imperishable crown. 26 Therefore I run thus: not with uncertainty. Thus I fight: not as one who beats the air. 27 But I discipline my body and bring it into subjection, lest, when I have preached to others, I myself should become disqualified."

1 Corinthians 9:24-27 (NKJV)

In the last two chapters, I shared seven steps with you in regards to getting out of *the rat race*. It is important to note that these are the vital steps to lead you into your *God Race* and help you obtain your prize. Life is a big race; an interesting one in which every individual gets to participate. Whether or not the race you are currently running is *The*

Rat Race or *The God Race*, I can assure you, you are indeed running a race.

The following are four special things to note regarding this race of life:

1. Everyone has their own, distinctive, starting point. The fact that we all entered this world at different times, through different parents and from different birth places, helps to buttress the fact that we cannot all be expected to start our race from the same starting points.

2. Everyone's race is unique. No two people are assigned to run the exact same race. Your *God Race* is about the unique calling God has designed for you to accomplish here on earth. If God allowed two people to be born into this world to fulfill the exact same assignment, one of the two would be unnecessary.

3. Everyone gets to run their race in their own unique lane. This is of great help since you do not have to deal with any kind of traffic or overcrowding in your lane. You do not have to compete with anyone for running space in your lane. As a matter of fact, in *God's Race*, you do not even compete with anyone at all.

4. Everyone's finish line is unique. Since your race is unique, your finish line is also unique. Just as you came into this world on your own, when it's time to leave, you have to do it on your own. This is why you cannot afford to use another man's clock (timing) to run your race. You must be able to accurately discern the sound of the gun to know when to start your race and the voice of your God ordained officials who will guide you through the race to the finish line.

Don't Look For Crowd Support

As I mentioned earlier, because everyone is busy running in their own unique race, you cannot afford to wait around looking for someone to give you the necessary encouragement or moral support to start running your race. If you currently happen to have someone in your life who motivates you to run, you should consider yourself blessed. Sometimes the race of life can be a lonely one as there are times when no one else is taking the same turn or going around the same corner that you are. You have to learn to motivate yourself to keep going.

In 1 Samuel 30:6, the bible tells of a man with no crowd support during a time he really needed it to get started on a new lap of his race.

"And David was greatly distressed; for the people spake of stoning him, because the soul of all the people was grieved, every man for his sons and for his daughters: but David encouraged himself in the LORD his God."   1 Samuel 30:6 *(KJV)*

On this particular occasion, not only was David without any crowd support, the people around him were actually at his throat and some of them wanted to stone him. Yet, the Bible states he encouraged himself in the Lord. Surely there will be times when you will need to encourage yourself in the Lord to get started on a course because you may not have any crowd support. On the other hand, the writer of the book of Hebrews lets us know in the first verse of the twelfth chapter that there is a crowd of witnesses in the heavens looking down and cheering us on. Though you may not be able to confirm this with your physical senses, you must believe it is true.

"Therefore we also, since we are surrounded by so great a cloud of witnesses, let us lay aside every weight, and the sin which so easily ensnares us, and let us run with endurance the race that is set before us..."   Hebrews 12:1 *(NKJV)*

Too many Christians are sitting in church pews Sunday after Sunday unwilling to get up and get in their *God Race*. They have been deceived to think it is enough to just come to church to listen to a preacher, who by the way is already running his *God Race*. If you have been one in this category, it's time to get up off your blessed assurance and go find your starting point. There is a race you must run and finish.

Taking The First Few Steps

A Chinese philosopher named Lao-tzu once said, "*A journey of a thousand miles begins with a single step.*" This is so true when it comes to *God's Race* and we are all called to run. You do not need a lot of energy for the first few steps. There isn't much resistance to stop your first few steps. You just need enough to overcome the physical force called *inertia*. "Inertia" can be defined as: *1. A tendency to do nothing or to remain unchanged such as with "bureaucratic inertia."* and *2. A property of matter by which it continues in its existing state of rest or uniform motion in a straight line, unless that state is changed by an external force. (Merriam-Webster dictionary)*

I have come to realize that apart from the physical resistance force, there are also other emotional/spiritual forces you may need to overcome in order to take the first few steps in your *God Race*. One, of such, is the issue of crowd support mentioned earlier. Another is the issue of desiring a certain amount of information about your *God Race*. Most of the people I have met who are immobile concerning their *God Race* claim they cannot start running because they do not have enough details about their specific race. You must understand that you do not need to know everything about the entire race to get started.

Another unique thing about the *God Race* is that many of the details concerning the race are unveiled as you run. The more you run the more you become informed about your race. Remember, at the beginning of the race, you do not know about the duration of your race or the exact location of the finish line. Yet you must be willing to take the first few steps off the starting blocks. This is why the *God Race* is also called the "Faith Race."

At this point, there is one very important tip I must give you is: Though you do not have all the details you might need for your race, there is One who does. This person knows the location of your starting blocks as well as your finish line. In order to start, run and finish your race well, you need to have a close relationship with this person. This person is Jesus. His presence and help is made manifest to you on the earth through the person of the Holy Spirit.

Prayer:

Heavenly Father, I pray for the true revelation of your Holy Spirit. Holy Spirit, I need you in my life. Please come, baptize me and fill me. Teach me to know you, listen to you and walk with you. Holy Spirit, please come and live inside of me in Jesus Name. Amen!

Chapter 7

STAYING ON COURSE

"Your ears shall hear a word behind you, saying, 'This is the way; walk in it.' Whenever you turn to the right hand or whenever you turn to the left."

Isaiah 30:21 *(NKJV)*

Our ability to hear the voice of God is so vital to experiencing success in the different areas of our life.

The wise man, Solomon, stated in Proverbs 16:25, *"There is a way that seems right to a man, But its end is the way of death."* The fact that you think you are on the right path does not necessarily mean you are. You have to be careful to know whose leadership you are following. Truly, there is nothing better than hearing the voice of the Lord whispering in your ears which way to go, particularly when dealing with something as important as your *God Race*.

Staying On The Path

It is one thing to start your race well; it's another to run the race well. In order to run well, it is important that you stay in your lane and on the right course. History reveals many who started their *God Race* very well but ended up aborting their race in the middle of it. Others ended up in wrong destinations because they were running in the wrong lane. You want to make sure that you stay on the right path.

> *...looking unto Jesus, the author and finisher of our faith, who for the joy that was set before Him endured the cross, despising the shame, and has sat down at the right hand of the throne of God."*

The key to staying on the right path is to maintain your focus on the One who already knows the path and can let you know if you are going off course. Jesus is not only the author and the finisher of our faith; He is also the one who designed our starting point and finish line of our *God Race*. Anyone who becomes proficient at keeping their eyes on Jesus will never stumble out of their lane nor faint during their race. For, to take your eyes off of Jesus is to risk stumbling or going off course.

May I remind you of the story of a man who had a unique opportunity to walk on water? Peter, one of the

Jesus' disciples, was quick to set off from the starting blocks. By the time one could say, "On your marks, get set…" Peter would be gone. Peter is a typical example of a prompt starter who would not allow any physical, emotional or spiritual *inertia* to keep him on the starting blocks. He also did not need crowd support to get going. He was ready to move with or without the support of his peers.

> "But straightway Jesus spake unto them, saying, 'Be of good cheer; it is I; be not afraid.' And Peter answered him and said, 'Lord, if it be thou, bid me come unto thee on the water.' And he said, 'Come.' And when Peter was come down out of the ship, he walked on the water, to go to Jesus. But when he saw the wind boisterous, he was afraid; and beginning to sink, he cried, saying, 'Lord, save me.' And immediately Jesus stretched forth his hand, and caught him, and said unto him, 'O thou of little faith, wherefore didst thou doubt?' And when they were come into the ship, the wind ceased."
>
> Matthew 14:27-32 (KJV)

Notice the bible clearly states that Peter started walking on water, meaning he was already running his race to finish his course which was to get to Jesus on the water. There was only one problem no one warned Peter about;

Peter did not know his success in completing his course was dependent on keeping his eyes on Jesus. The Bible lets us know that as soon as Peter took his eyes off Jesus focusing on the wind, be began to sink. The wind is a representation of life's challenges and the obstacles capable of distracting you from staying focused on your race. For instance, the wind could be family issues, financial issues, health issues or emotional issues. Many of these issues are orchestrated by the enemy of your soul to cause you distraction and thus abort your race.

Today, there are many of God's children who have been totally side tracked from their race. Some realize it and are trying to get back on course while others do not even realize they are off course. It is so important for you keep your eyes on Jesus by maintaining a healthy relationship with Him and the person of the Holy Spirit. Without this relationship, you stand little or no chance of staying on the right path.

As you are reading this book, if you are one who has suddenly realized you may have veered from your course, I have great news for you - it's not too late to get back on the path. Just like Peter, you too can cry out to the Lord to save you and stop you from sinking. Our Lord is faithful and loving. He will reach out to grab your hand and put you back on course. Notice that Peter eventually finished the course he started out to achieve, which was to walk on water to Jesus. Regardless of whether or not he started sinking, he still made it to the finish line, which was the arm of Jesus.

At this point, I want to encourage you to stop and confess this prayer: *"Lord, I agree that You are the author and finisher of my faith. I also believe that You know my beginning and ending points as well as the path I should follow. Now I surrender my plans, my will and my thoughts to You and ask You to lead me in the way I should go. I choose to trust You with all my heart that You will lead me in the right path. Lord, if I have been drifting away in recent times please grab me and put me back on the path. Thank You Holy Spirit for doing this for me in Jesus name! Amen!"*

Discipline & Diligence; The Power Twins

So far, I have shared a few truths with you from God's word on starting your race and staying on course. Now I want to show you some truths concerning maintaining your pace. Running is not necessarily fun for everyone. I know some of you love running and would do it every day, three times a day if you could. I'm sorry, but I am not one who loves running. When I run, it is primarily to exercise my body and stay in shape. When I run for a reasonable amount of time, I feel tired and my joints hurt. Rather than running, I mostly do a fast walk at the gym. I must admit, the reason I feel pain when I run is because I do not do it often enough.

It is true that the more you exercise your body, the fitter you become. My ability to run for a long period of time is dependent on two main factors: my willingness to discipline my physical body to get it in shape for running and the need to exercise diligently (not just once in a while). I suspect those disciplined and diligent enough to run daily do not hurt like I do when I run.

Paul's discussion about *The God Race* in 1 Corinthians 9:24-27; he uses the analogy of competitive athletics, like the Olympics, to emphasize we are to run with the aim to win. No one wins a race by accident; winning is intentional. You must have been training hard to condition your body to be at its peak performance in order to give all it takes for you to win the race. In other words, you cannot win a competitive race without applying the power of **discipline** and **diligence**. I call them the power twins.

"Do you not know that those who run in a race all run, but one receives the prize? Run in such a way that you may obtain it. And everyone who competes for the prize is temperate in all things. Now they do it to obtain a perishable crown, but we for an

imperishable crown. Therefore I run thus: not with uncertainty. Thus I fight: not as one who beats the air. But I discipline my body and bring it into subjection, lest, when I have preached to others, I myself should become disqualified."

1 Corinthians 9:24-27 (NKJV)

If you take a closer look at the twenty-seventh verse, you will see that Paul is clearly stating that the lack of discipline and diligence in the life of an athlete may not just cost them the highest medal (gold), it may actually lead to disqualification from the race. For example, a person that does not maintain lane discipline might run into another runner's path disrupting their race and could become disqualified as a result.

There are different dimensions of discipline necessary for running your *God Race*. I can put them in three basic categories: Spiritual Discipline, Emotional or Character Discipline, and Physical Discipline.

Physical Discipline:

Just as an athlete who runs in races, a believer in Christ also needs to have certain physical disciplines in place to ensure they remain healthy and fit for running their *God Race* all the way to the finish line. You need to discipline yourself to sleep right, eat right and exercise regularly. Remember that you only have one earth-suit and when it fails, you have to check out of this side of eternity. Many anointed people checked out prematurely because they neglected necessary physical disciplines. It is important for you to take this aspect of discipline very seriously especially if you intend to run well and make it to the finish line.

Emotional or Character Discipline:

Another very important area where you need discipline is your character as a runner. I believe your attitude in life has a lot to do with the altitude you can achieve in life. Anyone who wants to run their *God Race* well to the finish line must be willing to develop and demonstrate the Fruits of the Spirit. For example, an athlete that does not maintain lane discipline and keeps running into other people might be disqualified; particularly if the judges believe another runner was disrupted intentionally.

Many people today are deceived, thinking they are in competition with others while running their own race. This opens the door to negative character traits like jealousy, envy, strife and backbiting. Though most people involved in this kind of behavior would not admit it, the root is in their desire for others to fail so that they may succeed.

Other character flaws that can cause you to become disqualified during your race are anger, impatience and lack of self-control. Satan is crafty enough to explore the character flaws in the life of a person and use it to disqualify that person before they get to their finish line. There are many great achievers in various disciplines that started their race and ran it very well, and then one day, ended it in a very bad way because they lacked discipline in the area of character.

Spiritual Discipline:

This is the most vital area of discipline. I have come to realize, one's achievements in this area serves as their foundation for which to build physical and emotional discipline. Spiritual indiscipline usually results from a lack of control with the flesh and emotions. This is how carnal Christians are produced. However, those who learn to sow to their spirit through spiritual disciplines such as prayer, bible study and taking time to worship God will reap spiritual growth and stamina needed for their God race.

"⁷ Do not be deceived, God is not mocked; for whatever a man sows, that he will also reap. ⁸ For he who sows to his flesh will of the flesh reap corruption, but he who sows to the Spirit will of the Spirit reap everlasting life."

Galatians 6:7-8 (NKJV)

107

This is why, in 1 Corinthians 9:27, Paul talked about the need to buffet your body and bring it in to control so that you do not end up disqualified after you may have been running well. According to Paul, it is even possible to have preached to others encouraging them to start their race and run it yet end up becoming disqualified because of lacking spiritual indiscipline.

The Prize Comes With A Price

In truth, there is a price to pay for those serious about winning the prize reserved for making it to the finish line. One of my favorite things to say to myself when working out at the gym is, "No pain, no gain." I repeat it to myself particularly when my muscles start to ache. There is no athlete serious enough about winning a medal that does not take time to pay the price for ensuring they are in the shape to obtain it.

I remember listening to a preacher use the analogy of price tags on items in the store to teach about paying the necessary price to obtain what you want. Everything in a store is available to you. The issue is whether or not you are willing to pay the price printed on the tag. You must understand there is a price you need to pay to obtain the prize.

You are an answer to somebody's question. You are a solution to somebody's problem. Within the church I pastor, I see so many people around me filled with varying gifts. Some are called to the fivefold ministry while others are called to be great entrepreneurs and marketplace leaders. I always make it my duty to remind them all that none of them are a wondering generality, but rather each person is a meaningful specific.

You must understand that you *can* become all you are supposed to be. It is absolutely important that you pay the price necessary to get out of *The Rat Race* so that you may be launched into the more important *God Race* which has been preplanned for you since the beginning of time. For some it might take two or three years, for others it might take seven years to get out of *The Rat Race*; regardless of how long, I want to encourage you to start today!

Pay Now To Play Later

Now some people choose to start out their life playing and expect that one day, they will miraculously obtain the prize. This is not possible without paying a greater price later to compensate for the "playing" period. What we have done with credit cards and borrowed money says we want to "play now and pay later."

Whether you pay now or later, I guarantee that no matter what you do, you *will* pay. If you choose to play now then you sell your future away and you will pay in your old age when you are least able to afford it. Delayed payment always costs you more. If you can pay now and play later, you will best enjoy being free financially to find your purpose. In life, you have to learn to pay your price early so that you may play later.

This truth can be illustrated by simply considering the difference between the person getting an education early in life and the one waiting until the age of forty to do so. No doubt the one choosing to pay the price earlier ends up playing later while the other is busy paying. Whether you pay now or pay later, you will surely need to pay the price necessary to obtain the prize you desire. Your God Race is the most important race you will ever run and it is worth all that you can give to it. If you have not already started paying the price, I urge you to start today.

I really believe that time is short. As we are moving closer and closer to the last days, we need to get our acts together so we can be useful to Almighty God during these times. We can't be useful stuck in *the rat race*. Everybody on earth is here on purpose for a purpose! You must get out of the maze and find your God given purpose. Every single one of us is special to God. Every single one of us is significant to God. That is why God saw to it that there would be no duplicates. There is no other person on the face of the earth exactly like you. You have been uniquely gifted.

Remember Romans 8:19? *"The whole earth is in earnest expectation and eagerly waits for the sons of God to show up."* The word "sons" in this translation is including all mankind, not just males. This means His sons and daughters. The word "son" here is being used as an example of a certain level of maturity. You can be a baby, you can be a child, but the description "son" means you have come up to a maturity with the Father.

Prayer:

Father, I pray I come to know my purpose and unique race. I pray against laziness, procrastination or any other things hindering me from starting or running my race today. Help me to stop settling for less in life but rather to go for all You have pre-planned for my life in Jesus Name. Amen!

Finishing Strong

Chapter 8

FINISHING STRONG

"Arise, shine; for your light has come! And the glory of the Lord is risen upon you."

Isaiah 60:1 (NKJV)

It is one thing to start a race well. It is another to run well and yet another to finish well. The most important part of a race that really determines who gets the prize is the finish. Regardless of whether or not you started strong, you must strive to finish strong especially if you are serious about winning your prize.

Know It's A Marathon

In the year 2005, I read a powerful book by Steve Farrah called "Finishing Strong." In his book, I learned that our race in life is not a one hundred meter dash or a two hundred meter sprint where the finish line is in close sight. Rather it is a marathon.

In the last chapter, I mentioned the fact that time is short and your world is waiting for you to pay your price. In his epistle to the church in Rome, Paul made a statement to support this truth:

"For the earnest expectation of the creation eagerly waits for the revealing of the sons of God. For the creation was subjected to futility, not willingly, but because of Him who subjected it in hope..."   Romans 8:19-20 (NKJV)

Notice the last phrase of verse twenty, *"but because of Him who subjected it in hope."* In hope of what? That the sons of God would show up to make a difference! I want you to know that the world is waiting for you to show up and make an impact.

On the 11th of July, 1995, my wife and I were at a Sunday morning meeting at Victory Church in London. A well respected visiting evangelist and prophet named Dick Mills was ministering. He called my wife and me out of the audience to give us a prophetic word. He began to prophecy the very things that are happening to us today. He went on to describe what the Lord would do with our lives. He told us the answers the Lord had for us and the wisdom He would give us to fulfill our destiny and purpose. That was in 1995. It wasn't until nine years later before any of these things began to manifest in our lives. But we never gave up hope that the Lord would bring us to our destiny. You also must not give up hope that the Lord will bring you to your destiny if you stay passionate about getting there. He put gifts and talents in you. Through those He wants to get you out of *the rat race* and into your purpose.

Stay In Your Lane

As mentioned earlier, an important thing to note about *The God Race* is that we all get to run in different lanes. No two people have been called to do exactly the same thing in the same way. For example, every Pastor that is truly called of God has certain unique aspects of their God given vision. For this reason it is unfair for congregants to compare pastors or put one pastor under pressure to be like another one they know. *"Not that I have already attained, or am already perfected; but I press on, that I may lay hold of that for which Christ Jesus has also laid hold of me. Brethren, I do not count myself to have apprehended; but one thing I do, forgetting those things which are behind and reaching forward to those things which are ahead, I press toward the goal for the prize of the upward call of God in Christ Jesus."*

Philippians 3:12-14 (NKJV)

The closer you walk with Jesus, the more you get to know Him. The more you know Him, the more you get to know yourself. Our intimacy with Christ helps us to discover more about ourselves including the unique qualities and tasks we have been assigned.

Paul got to a place in his walk with Christ where he received a clear understanding of what he had to do with his life. He was willing to put everything else aside to pursue the "one thing" he was sure was his assignment in life. He wasn't trying to do ten things or five or even two at a time. Rather he was focused on doing "one thing."

Many of us today make the mistake of moving from one thing to another as we encounter a number of issues, such as boredom, obstacles or becoming enticed by the success someone else seems to be experiencing with what they are doing. It is important that you do not do this, as it might mean going out your lane while in the middle of your race. Not only could this lead to disqualification from the race you're in but it can also cause you to end up at the wrong destination. Whatever you do during your *God Race*, please ensure that you stay in your lane. Though you might be tired or discouraged, if you stay in your lane and keep on moving, even at a slow pace, you will eventually make it to the finish line successfully.

Paul knew he was primarily called to minister the gospel to the Gentiles; not to the Jews like Peter and some of the other Apostles. He made this clear in many of his epistles, including the one he wrote to the believers in Galatia, Ephesus, and to Timothy his spiritual son.

"But when it pleased God, who separated me from my mother's womb and called me through His grace, to reveal His Son in me, that I might **preach Him among the Gentiles,** *I did not immediately confer with flesh and blood, nor did I go up to Jerusalem to those who were apostles before me; but I went to Arabia, and returned again to Damascus."*

Galatians 1:15-17 (NKJV)

"To me, who am less than the least of all the saints, this grace was given, that I should **preach** *among the* **Gentiles** *the unsearchable riches of Christ…"* Ephesians 3:8 (NKJV)

"…but has now been revealed by the appearing of our Savior Jesus Christ, who has abolished death and brought life and immortality to light through the gospel, to which I was **appointed a preacher, an apostle, and a teacher of the Gentiles.** *For this reason I*

also suffer these things; nevertheless I am not ashamed, for I know whom I have believed and am persuaded that He is able to keep what I have committed to Him until that Day."

2 Timothy 1:10-12 (NKJV)

Paul would have aborted his race if he allowed the opposition, trials and tribulations experienced to cause him to change his ministry focus. He could have decided to change lanes in the middle of the race which would have resulted in him not completing his race. Thank God this was not the case. Thank God he stayed in his lane and completed his race regardless of every obstacle, opposition and temptations of the enemy. Paul was able to one day declare that he had made it to the finish line.

*"...for I am already being poured out as a drink offering, and the time of my departure is at hand. I have fought the good fight, **I have finished the race**, I have kept the faith, Finally, there is laid up for me the crown of righteousness, which the Lord, the righteous Judge, will give to me on that Day, and not to me only but also to all who have loved His appearing."*   2 Timothy 4:6-8 (NKJV)

Unique Finish Line

Paul was indeed a very unique man amongst the New Testament saints because he was one out of many that was able to testify he had made it to the finish line. We know many of the others did well and ran a good race but we cannot find any writing to confirm they believed they made it to the finish line. The finish line for your *God Race* is just as unique as the actual race you have to run. The only person who knows your finish line is Christ Himself. He is the only one that can confirm to you if and when you've made it to that point.

Paul was highly privileged to have this classified information confirmed to him as well as to have enough time to document it in his letters to Timothy, his spiritual son. I believe this was documented for our benefit so those of us who would be alive many generations later could see that it *is* possible to discover our *God Race*, run well, and stay in our lane for a strong finish. Remember that your *God Race* is a type of marathon and not a short dash. It is important that you keep your eyes on Jesus and trust Him to help you make it all the way to the finish line. My prayer is that you and I make it.

The Crown

Another thing we must remember to keep in our spiritual sight is the stake of the prize at the end of our race. In Paul's letter to the church in Corinth (1 Corinthians

9:24-27), he mentioned being aware there was an imperishable crown God would put on the head of the one that runs well and finishes strong. This, he said, was to be the motivating factor for all runners, same as the gold medal is the motivating factor for athletes in our world today. To lose sight of the prize is to lose sight of the reason behind running well and staying in the race until you make it to the finish line.

Our world has seen many saints who were able to get out of *The Rat Race* and discover their unique *God Race*. Many even went on to start their *God Race* well and ran at a good pace. They ran so well they convinced many of the other believers in Christ, who were alive in their time that they were going to make it all the way. But something happened and they fell or became disqualified. I honestly believe the primary reason they fell short of the finish line is because at some point during the race they took their eyes off Jesus and the prize. Satan is very crafty and good at bringing distractions to cause us to lose our focus of Christ and the crown.

May I remind you of the story of Elijah and Elisha? Elijah promised to grant Elisha's request of the double portion anointing only if he could stay focused till the end. Elisha was clear about what he wanted from Elijah. He had served his master faithfully for many years and he was now in the final lap of his race to receive his reward. Elisha was so determined to get the prize, he ignored Elijah's suggestion to return home – once at Bethel and a second time at the Jordan. The key to getting the prize, in this case Elijah's mantle, was to stay focused on Elijah till the very last second before he was taken up to the heavens by God.

*"Then Elijah said to him, 'Stay here, please, for the LORD has sent me on to the Jordan.' But he said, 'As the LORD lives, and as your soul lives, I will not leave you!' So the two of them went on. And fifty men of the sons of the prophets went and stood facing them at a distance, while the two of them stood by the Jordan. Now Elijah took his mantle, rolled it up, and struck the water; and it was divided this way and that, so that the two of them crossed over on dry ground. And so it was, when they had crossed over, that Elijah said to Elisha, 'Ask! What may I do for you, before I am taken away from you?' Elisha said, 'Please let a double portion of your spirit be upon me.' So he said, 'You have asked a hard thing. Nevertheless, **if you see me when I am taken from you, it shall be so for you**; but if not, it shall not be so.' Then it happened, as they continued on and talked, that suddenly a chariot of fire appeared with horses of fire, and separated the two of them; and Elijah went up by a whirlwind into heaven. And Elisha saw it, and he cried out, 'My father, my father, the chariot of Israel and its horsemen!' So he saw him no more. And he took hold of his own clothes and tore them into two pieces. He also*

took up the mantle of Elijah that had fallen from him, and went back and stood by the bank of the Jordan."

2 Kings 2:6-13 (NKJV)

Just as Elisha had to stay focused on Elijah and the mantle till the very second Elijah was taken up, so must you and I stay focused on Jesus and the crown if we are going to receive it. We cannot afford to be distracted by the things of this world. Like I always say to men, we must stay away from lust for girls, gold, and glory. Like Paul, we must be willing to discipline our flesh and bring it under subjection in order to ensure that we are not disqualified.

Prayer:

Holy Spirit, the bible states that You are my Comforter and the One called to walk alongside me. I pray for Your guidance and leadership as I run my race. Please help me to stay focused, to stay in my lane and maintain a good pace. I pray I will not fall or fail that I may finish my race in Jesus name! Amen!

MY VISION OF THE FINISH LINE

In the early hours of Tuesday, September 6th, I experienced a vision from the Lord. In this vision, I saw myself looking at a very large mountain with snow covering the top. It was a beautiful sight. Then I heard a voice say, "Let me show you a different view."

In a split second I began to see a wider view of the mountain as though I was pulled back away from the mountain or the mountain was pushed away from me. As this view continued to widen, I noticed more lands, seas and the sky. From where I was and in what seemed like just a couple of seconds, I was able to see the entire globe.

For a moment, I began to wonder where I was that I could see this awesome view. Just before I could take it all in, I was led by the same being who suggested I see the different view earlier. The interesting thing was that I did not see the being nor hear his voice, which was not really audible; however I could perceive it, somehow, in my spirit.

Then I noticed I started travelling very fast in what seemed like a downward direction – like a dive. In another split second the thought occurred to me that maybe I was heading for hell. That scared me, so I tried to communicate with the being to tell him that I did not want to go in that direction. Again, without uttering a word audibly, I could tell he was telling me not to worry. We were not going to hell.

Almost instantly, I started to notice lights in the horizon. The lights looked like stars in a distant galaxy. We seemed to have been travelling so fast yet slowed, because in another split second, I was beginning to see the particular lights that we were heading towards more clearly. It seemed in another split second I could see prisms of colors and could instantly tell it was a place. It was a very beautiful place full of bright lights and bright colors. It was something I'd never seen before.

Again, almost immediately after this, understanding came to me; I realized it must be heaven. This instantly brought fear of the possibility of not being able to return back to earth (home) if I went further. I immediately communicated to the being with me that I was scared and needed to go back to have my wife hold me – I needed to be sure I would be able to go back home. Please note, I could not see this being yet perceived his presence. I also noticed I was not uttering audible words but seemed to be communicating via my spirit. I believe he must have been an angel.

Instantly I woke up in my bed, into a state of consciousness and ask my sleeping wife to please hold me. As soon as I felt her arms around me, I decided to close my eyes again with the aim to go back to the place I saw earlier in my dream. Unfortunately, the being taking me on this trip was gone. I instantly realized I could no longer go back into the realm I was in before and that my fear of not coming back had caused the experience to end. I tried hard with my eyes closed to go back but nothing happened.

Later, I woke my wife up to tell her what had happened. Initially she laughed at me, wondering why I got scared and came back to ask her to hold me. She let up when she noticed I was very upset.

I am sharing this experience with you to let you know that Heaven is real. I believe that through this experience, I was granted the opportunity to see a glimpse of the place all Christians staying with Christ to the end will go.

My brothers and sisters, this is the ultimate prize. All I have been sharing with you in this book, with regards to getting out of *The Rat Race* of life and entering *The God Race* of life, is about making it to Heaven and getting your reward. That is the place where the crown will be given. Making heaven must be the ultimate desire of our hearts and hence we must be willing to pay whatever price is necessary to get there.

May I remind you that your *God Race* does not have to be a full-time fivefold ministry! Not all of us are called to serve God from behind pulpits. Some of us are called to be witnesses for Christ in the marketplace. Your *God Race* always has to do with fulfilling the unique assignment of God for your life. Whether you are called to be a banker, engineer, teacher, doctor or builder, ensure you do not spend the rest of your life working for money. Rather get free from *The Rat Race* and enter your *God Race*. Use your occupation, business or gifting to win souls and disciple them for Christ. I can assure you, not only will you make it into Heaven; you will also receive your crown in Jesus Name. Amen!

DANIEL OLUGBENGA MATEOLA

The Redemption Buffet

Possessing All Jesus Died To Recover For You

Foreword by Pastor Matthew Ashimolowo

FOR A COMPLETE LIST OF
BOOKS AND RESOURCES BY
APOSTLE DANIEL MATEOLA

CONTACT

PERAZIM INTERNATIONAL CHRISTIAN CENTRE
820 SOUTH CENTRAL AVE
MEDFORD OR 97504
(541) 776-8532
or
info@danielmateolaministries.org

Made in the USA
Charleston, SC
22 May 2012